PROGRESSIVE ERA
LEADERS

Monika Davies

Consultant

Brian Allman
Social Studies Teacher and Milken Educator
Upshur County Schools, West Virginia

Publishing Credits

Rachelle Cracchiolo, *M.S.Ed., Publisher*
Emily R. Smith, *M.A.Ed., VP of Content Development*
Véronique Bos, *Creative Director*
Dona Herweck Rice, *Senior Content Manager*
Dani Neiley, *Associate Editor*
Robin Erickson, *Art Director*

Image Credits: p1, Library of Congress [LC-USZ6-1820]; p2, 26, LOC [LC-DIG-hec-30267]; p4 (from top) LOC [LC-USZ62-132336], [LC-USZ62-37937], [LC-DIG-ppmsca-38818]; p5, (from top) LOC [LC-USZ62-137950], LOC [LC-USZC2-6247], The University of Chicago Library, LOC [LC-USZ62-109793], LOC [LC-DIG-ppmsca-36082], LOC [LC-DIG-npcc-26147]; p6, LOC [LC-DIG-ppmsca-36082]; p7, LOC [LC-USZC4-494]; p8, LOC [LC-USZC2-6247]; p9, US National Archives; p10, LOC [LC-USZ62-132336] p11, LOC [LC-USZ62-97324]; p12, LOC [LC-USZ62-53912]; p13, (top) LOC [LC-DIG-ppmsca-25884], (bottom) LOC [LC-USZ62-51280]; p14, LOC [LC-DIG-npcc-26147]; p15, Alamy Stock Photo; p16, LOC [LC-USZ62-137950]; p17, (top) LOC [LC-DIG-nclc-02867], (bottom) LOC [LC-DIG-nclc-01581]; pp18–19, The University of Chicago Library; p20, LOC [LC-DIG-ppmsca-38818]; p22, LOC [LC-USZ62-109793]; p23, LOC [LC-USZ62-57860]; p24, LOC [LC-USZ62-37937]; p25, LOC [LC-USZ62-31799]; p27, Getty Images; p28, Carrie Chapman Catt Collection, Bryn Mawr College Library; p29, (top) LOC [LC-DIG-ppmsca-25884], (middle) LOC [LC-USZ6-1820]; all other images from iStock and/or Shutterstock

Library of Congress Cataloging-in-Publication Data

Names: Davies, Monika, author.
Title: Progressive Era leaders / Monika Davies.
Description: Huntington Beach, CA : Teacher Created Materials, [2021] | Includes index. | Audience: Grades 4-6 | Summary: "Between around 1890 and 1920, the Progressive Era saw the United States become a more democratic, safer, and greater nation. Many people led the charge for change and made progress possible. They exposed corruption, secured the vote for women, and spoke up for citizens with no voice. They also forced the government to work for its people. They changed the United States for the better. Let's meet the movers and shakers of the Progressive Era"-- Provided by publisher.
Identifiers: LCCN 2021029541 (print) | LCCN 2021029542 (ebook) | ISBN 9781425850647 (paperback) | ISBN 9781425834449 (ebook)
Subjects: LCSH: Progressivism (United States politics)--Juvenile literature. | United States--Biography--Juvenile literature. | United States--History--1865-1921--Juvenile literature. | United States--Politics and government--1865-1933--Juvenile literature.
Classification: LCC E663 .D38 2021 (print) | LCC E663 (ebook) | DDC 973.8092/2--dc23
LC record available at https://lccn.loc.gov/2021029541
LC ebook record available at https://lccn.loc.gov/2021029542

TCM
Teacher Created Materials

5482 Argosy Avenue
Huntington Beach, CA 92649
www.tcmpub.com
ISBN 978-1-4258-5064-7
© 2022 Teacher Created Materials, Inc.

Table of Contents

Progressive Voices

The Progressive Era was a time of great change in America. Lasting from around 1890 to 1920, this era was a period of big social **movements**. It brought major political **reforms**. In this time, many groups worked to make the United States a safer, more democratic nation.

It was an era defined by movements. Governments were held more accountable for their actions. Women's **suffrage** came to be. Corruption was uncovered and stamped out. Powerful voices spoke up for civil rights.

The people who led the charge for change made progress possible. Some of the most famous people in American history lived during this era. They worked to create a reformed United States. Some were presidents, many were writers, and a few were dynamic public speakers.

But what was most important about them was how they spoke up for the people. They forced the government to work for its people. Many people say they changed the United States for the better. These were the leaders of the Progressive Era.

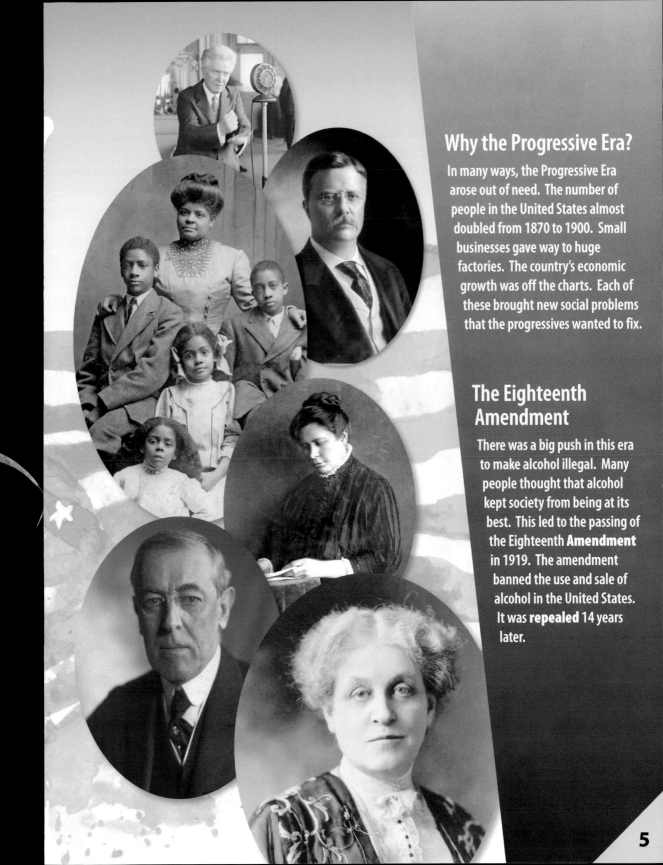

Why the Progressive Era?

In many ways, the Progressive Era arose out of need. The number of people in the United States almost doubled from 1870 to 1900. Small businesses gave way to huge factories. The country's economic growth was off the charts. Each of these brought new social problems that the progressives wanted to fix.

The Eighteenth Amendment

There was a big push in this era to make alcohol illegal. Many people thought that alcohol kept society from being at its best. This led to the passing of the Eighteenth **Amendment** in 1919. The amendment banned the use and sale of alcohol in the United States. It was **repealed** 14 years later.

The Presidents

With the onset of the Progressive Era, two U.S. leaders stood out. Each believed his reforms would help the American people.

Theodore Roosevelt (1901–1909)

[*"A great democracy must be progressive, or it will soon cease to be great or a democracy."*]

At 42, Theodore Roosevelt was the youngest person to become president. He inspired a nation to ask for more from its leaders.

As president, Roosevelt had a very progressive agenda. One of his goals was to break up business **monopolies**. These are companies with complete control of certain goods in the market. First, the company can set prices for the items it makes. Second, product **innovation** is unlikely. A company is less likely to try new things when it doesn't have to compete. The company becomes **complacent**, and growth may stop. Many people thought monopolies hurt the country.

In 1890, the Sherman Antitrust Act was passed. It gave the government power to break up **trusts** that interfered with trade. But the act had rarely been put to use. In 1902, Roosevelt used the act to break up a railroad **conglomerate**. He asked the Justice Department to prosecute them. After two long years, he won the case. Over the next seven years, 43 other suits were brought against companies. For his work, Roosevelt earned the nickname "Trust-Buster."

Mediator

Roosevelt was the first president to take the side of laborers in a dispute. There was a coal strike in 1902. The miners wanted shorter hours and higher pay. Roosevelt **mediated** a meeting between the owners and the workers. He was also the first president to choose a peaceful path instead of sending troops to break up a strike.

Roosevelt's Words

Roosevelt was a great speaker who was known for creating words and phrases like these:

- A *bully pulpit* is a position that allows a person to talk about issues and raise awareness.
- A *square deal* means a fair bargain.
- A *muckraker* looks into and writes about corruption in politics and business.

This 1889 anti-monopoly cartoon contributed to the passage of the Sherman Antitrust Act.

7

Woodrow Wilson (1913–1921)

> *"I not only use all the brains that I have but all that I can borrow."*

Woodrow Wilson was the 28th president and an **idealist**. Even though he and Roosevelt weren't in the same political party, they both held progressive ideals.

In 1913, Wilson signed an act to create the Federal Reserve System, also known as the "Fed." This is the central bank of the United States. Before the Fed, the U.S. economy was unstable. Bank failures and public panics were common. The Fed brought stability.

The Fed still supervises banks. It makes sure banks comply with laws and **regulations**.

Bringing on Brandeis

In 1916, Wilson named Louis Brandeis to the U.S. Supreme Court. Brandeis caught Wilson's eye by fighting against the abuse of child workers and women. But many people fought the appointment. They said he was too radical and too progressive. Some were opposed to Brandeis because he was Jewish American. At this time, there was a great deal of prejudice in society against Jewish people.

The Nineteenth Amendment to the Constitution was added while Wilson was president. This gave women the right to vote. At first, Wilson was not a supporter of suffrage. After World War I, he changed his mind. He saw how important women were to the war effort. In 1918, Wilson made a speech to Congress. He said, "We have made partners of the women in this war." He also declared women should have "a partnership of privilege and right."

The amendment was not passed after his speech. It took another year of work. But in 1920, it was finally **ratified** while Wilson was still president.

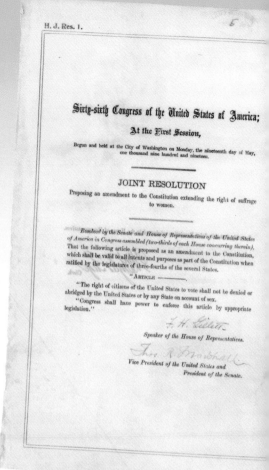

▲ the Nineteenth Amendment

▼ Suffragists protest in front of the White House in 1918.

The Muckrakers

Roosevelt called some writers "muckrakers." He meant this negatively. These journalists were known for writing **exposés**. By writing about corruption, they brought attention to problems and sparked change.

Upton Sinclair

> *"I aimed at the public's heart, and by accident I hit it in the stomach."*

Upton Sinclair was perhaps the best-known muckraker. This comes directly from his novel *The Jungle*. It uncovered the brutal working conditions of Chicago stockyards.

Sinclair spent weeks researching his novel in Packingtown. This was the name for the meatpacking plants in Chicago. He wanted his novel to center on the **exploitation** of immigrants. Readers focused more on this information:

> *"The meat would be shoveled into carts, and the man who did the shoveling would not trouble to lift out a rat even when he saw one…There was no place for the men to wash their hands before they ate their dinner, and so they…[washed] them in the water that was to be ladled into the sausage."*

Readers could not believe what they read. Was this really what happened to the meat they ate?

Sinclair's *The Jungle* sparked a public outcry. People demanded stronger food regulations to protect them. Roosevelt listened. In 1906, the Meat Inspection Act and the Pure Food and Drug Act were passed.

▼ Packingtown, around 1909

The Acts of 1906

The Meat Inspection Act made sure that livestock was marked correctly before sale. The processing of the livestock also had to be clean and sanitary. The Pure Food and Drug Act made sure that food and drugs were properly labeled, too. It also outlawed the making and selling of poisonous foods and drugs.

Pen Pals

After *The Jungle* shocked readers, Sinclair wrote a letter to Roosevelt. In it, he described how to fix the meat industry. He suggested that any investigators should wear disguises. That would allow them to get a clear view of what was really happening.

Ida Tarbell

"I was not a writer, and I knew it. [But] there was my habit of steady, painstaking work...And perhaps I could learn to write."

Thank You, Mark Twain

Author Mark Twain played a role in Tarbell's exposé. Henry H. Rogers was an executive at the Standard Oil Company. He was also friends with Twain. Twain introduced Tarbell and Rogers. His open talks with Tarbell confirmed what she found. Rogers helped her take down his company without realizing what he was doing.

Revenge?

Tarbell had a good reason to go after Standard Oil. Many years before, the company had put her father out of business. He was an oil producer and refiner. When Tarbell was about 14, Rockefeller bought out many small-time oil producers. Her family struggled financially. The memory of being wronged never left her.

She was an investigator first and a writer second. That is how Ida Tarbell may have defined herself. But during her career, she was able to combine both skills. She is best known for her series of articles called *The History of the Standard Oil Company*. Her articles were published as a book in 1904. Through her story, she took down a corporate giant.

By 1900, the Standard Oil Company controlled 90 percent of the oil produced in the United States. This sort of monopoly was unfair. But their **unethical** practices were not publicly known. Tarbell spent almost two years researching her story. She dug through public records. She combed through old newspapers.

▲ This 1904 cartoon shows a Standard Oil octopus strangling businesses and government buildings.

THE HISTORY OF
THE STANDARD
OIL COMPANY

BY

IDA M. TARBELL

AUTHOR OF
THE LIFE OF ABRAHAM LINCOLN, THE LIFE OF NAPOLEON BONAPARTE,
AND MADAME ROLAND: A BIOGRAPHICAL STUDY

ILLUSTRATED WITH PORTRAITS
PICTURES AND DIAGRAMS

VOLUME ONE

NEW YORK
McCLURE, PHILLIPS & CO.
MCMV

Tarbell's exposé started as a **serial** in a magazine. Each piece covered the company's inner workings. She also did a profile on its founder, John D. Rockefeller. She called him "money-mad."

Many people read her words. They spoke out against the Standard Oil Company. In 1906, the company was charged under the Sherman Antitrust Act. Five years later, the company was dissolved.

The Reformers

Reform is about changes to try to improve a situation. The following people knew their country needed reforms. They were not afraid to help make those changes happen.

Robert M. La Follette

[
"The will of the people shall be the law of the land."
]

A progressive leader, Robert M. La Follette changed how the political game was played. Nicknamed "Fighting Bob," he was a three-time governor of Wisconsin and a U.S. senator.

In 1891, La Follette was practicing law in Madison, Wisconsin. A political leader offered him money if he would change the outcome of a case. La Follette was angry. He wanted to speak out against corrupt politicians. He became a popular speaker and drew big crowds. People listened to him.

Nine years later, when he became governor, he pushed for reforms. He started what he called a "roll call." In it, he listed all the legislators who opposed his bills in their districts. This persuaded many of them to vote for his reforms.

In 1906, La Follette became a U.S. senator. He was known for not being under the control of big businesses. From his position of power, he pushed for the breaking up of trusts. He also promoted labor regulations.

 This 1911 cartoon praises La Follette's reforms.

Referendum & Initiative

During this time, two important voting changes came to be. One is the *referendum*, and the other is the *initiative*. The first is when people can vote for or against a law about a specific issue. The second is a process. It gives people the chance to petition for a vote on a law or a change to the Constitution. Both are needed in democracies. They give voters power.

Recall Elections

Recall elections also came out of this era of change. They give people the power to recall, or remove, elected officials before their terms are done. A recall makes sure officials work for the public and not for their political parties or for themselves. In most places, recall elections are not common, but some officials have been recalled over the years.

Florence Kelley

A woman "must be more steady...
or more skilled, or more cheap
in order to have the same chance
of employment" as a man.

In the late 1800s, working conditions were bad for everyone, but they were worse for women and children. This needed to be changed. But change doesn't happen unless someone speaks up. Workers needed someone on their side. Florence Kelley was that person.

Kelley spent most of her life speaking up for working women and children. In 1892, she was hired to study Chicago slums and the working conditions in sweatshops. Her report was meant to focus on child labor.

A Hull House Resident

In 1891, Kelley moved to Chicago. There, she became a resident of Hull House. Its purpose was to provide aid for the neighborhood. Jane Addams, who later won a Nobel Peace Prize, founded Hull House. It was there that Kelley began her tireless efforts to help workers.

The NCL's Purpose

The NCL was founded in 1899 to protect workers. It focused on proper working conditions. These included fair minimum wages and limited working hours. It gave a "white label," as they called it, to businesses with safe and fair work policies. The NCL asked the public only to support businesses that had earned these white labels.

Kelley's findings paved the way for the Illinois Factory Act of 1893. She proposed that children under the age of 14 should not work in factories. Kelley also thought the number of hours women had to work in a day should be reduced.

When the act passed, she was named the chief factory inspector for Illinois. She made sure the laws that she helped put in place were followed. Six years later, Kelley took on another key role. She was named the first general secretary of the National Consumers League (NCL). Until her death in 1932, she kept supporting those who needed someone to fight for them.

A 14-year-old girl works in a Texas factory. ▶

▼ This 1909 photo shows children standing on machines to fix broken threads.

Ida B. Wells

[*"The way to right wrongs is to turn the light of truth upon them."*]

History is host to only a few truly fearless leaders. You can count Ida B. Wells as one of them. Born in 1862, Wells was the oldest of eight children. She was first a teacher, and then she became a journalist.

▲ Wells and her children in 1909

Wells wrote this letter to a famous Black author in 1915. ▶

Phone Douglas 153

The Negro Fellowship League
3005 State Street
Chicago

May. 18, 1915.

Mr. Charles W. Chestnutt,

Cleveland Ohio,

Dear Mr. Chestnutt:-

As you doubtless know by report from Mr. Trotter when he was on his western tour, we have a local branch of the Equal Rights League in Chicago. We had much enthusiasm and a crowded meeting while he was here, but in the propaganda work we very much need some other stimulus.

The organization has decided to give a dinner about the 10th or 11th of June and it unanimously voted to invite you to be our chief speaker. We want especially to bring home to our people the necessity of uniting their forces in order to win the new birth of freedom, and we must have some one to deliver this old message in a new dress so that it will arrest and hold them.

We are too new an organization to have any money in the treasury. We can only guarantee your expenses and entertainment. Will you be willing to come over in Macedonia and help us? Knowing you as well as I do, I believe you will come to the rescue and I am not hesitating to send out the call.

Please let me know as soon as possible and believe me to be,

Yours in the interest of the race,

Ida B. Wells Barnett

Wells became co-owner of the newspaper *Memphis Free Speech*. She wrote on a variety of issues affecting the Black community. Her words were eloquent and fiery.

In 1892, three of her friends were victims of a mob lynching. Enraged, Wells began a campaign of articles against lynching. While out of town, her office was raided by a mob. Instead of returning home, Wells broadened her campaign. She traveled across the country and across the sea to England. There, she continued her anti-lynching campaign to great success.

Wells was an active reformer. She helped found the National Association for the Advancement of Colored People (NAACP). She also fought for women's suffrage. Wells was not one to stand by when **injustice** happened. She was a fearless crusader.

A Fighter

Years before Rosa Parks, Wells also refused to give up her seat for a white man. In 1884, at the age of 22, she was ordered to give up her first-class train seat to a white passenger. The conductor tried to drag her out of the seat—so she bit his hand! She later sued the railroad company and won the case. The Supreme Court of Tennessee reversed the decision.

Importance of Names

In the 1800s, it was almost unheard of for a woman to keep her last name when she got married. But when Wells married in 1895, she chose to keep her name and hyphenate it with her husband's. She began introducing herself as Ida B. Wells-Barnett.

▼ **Wells's business card**

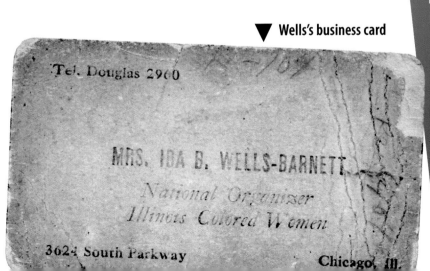

Tel. Douglas 2960

MRS. IDA B. WELLS-BARNETT

National Organizer
Illinois Colored Women

3024 South Parkway   Chicago, Ill.

W. E. B. Du Bois

[*"For the problem of the twentieth century is the problem of the color line."*]

William Edward Burghardt Du Bois was a strong voice for civil rights. In 1899, Du Bois published *The Philadelphia Negro: A Social Study*. It was the first case study of a Black community in the United States. It also put his name on the map. After that, Du Bois continued to write about Black life.

Du Bois vs. Washington

Du Bois's name is often linked with Booker T. Washington's. They were both well-known Black activists at the turn of the twentieth century. However, they had opposing views on how Black people should overcome inequalities. Washington told Black Americans to work hard to win the respect of white people. Du Bois disagreed. He believed that Black people needed to take action and protest for change to happen.

Overdue Honor

In 2013, long after his death, Du Bois received an honor. The University of Pennsylvania made him an honorary professor. He had been an effective teacher there. He worked as an assistant lecturer. But he was never hired full-time. His work in sociology and civil rights was inspiring to many people of his time. He still inspires people.

His famous book, *The Souls of Black Folk*, was released in 1903. "America is not another word for Opportunity to all her sons," he wrote. Du Bois wanted Black Americans to break down racial barriers. At the time, his writing shocked many people. Today, his words show great insight.

In 1909, he helped create the NAACP. But Du Bois found the NAACP too moderate. He left the organization in 1934.

During his lifetime, Du Bois stood up for what he knew was right and stuck to his strong opinions. Many people found him controversial. But his writing and work for civil rights had a big impact then and live on today. He is now thought of as perhaps the most important Black protest leader of his time.

THE SOULS OF BLACK FOLK

W.E.B. Du BOIS

The Suffragists

Once upon an era, voting was not an equal right for men and women. Women had to fight for their right to a ballot.

Carrie Chapman Catt

[*"We women demand an equal voice; we shall accept nothing less."*]

Every movement needs a leader. For the women's suffrage movement, Carrie Chapman Catt was at the helm.

Catt began as an Iowa law clerk before becoming an educator. Her bright confidence quickly secured her a superintendent position. She was one of the first women to earn this job.

In 1887, she began working with a group called the Iowa Woman Suffrage Association. Three years later, she became president of an even larger group. It was called National American Woman Suffrage Association (NAWSA). But when her husband became ill, she stepped down.

Catt returned to the group in 1915. At the time, NAWSA was divided. It needed guidance. Catt was the answer. She was a tireless worker and very organized. And her speeches got attention.

The next year, Catt's "Winning Plan" was put in place. It was designed to support suffrage at both the state *and* the federal levels. This was the final push needed to get the vote.

Slowly, NAWSA received state support. Then, Congress was on its side. In 1920, the Nineteenth Amendment was finally added to the U.S. Constitution. Thanks in part to Catt, women could finally vote.

▼ 1920 newspaper announces ratification of the Nineteenth Amendment.

An Unusual Marriage Plan

In 1890, Carrie Chapman married George W. Catt. They made an unusual deal when they married. They decided that she would have four months every year to dedicate to women's suffrage. George Catt was supportive of his wife's work as a suffragist. When he died in 1905, he left her with enough money to continue her work for reforms.

League of Women Voters

After women won the right to vote, Catt proposed that NAWSA be reorganized and renamed. It became the League of Women Voters (LWV). The LWV became a **nonpartisan** group. It encourages people to take an active role in their government. The LWV is still active.

No. 27,880. Entered as second-class matter post office Washington, D. C.

SUFFRAGE PROCLAIMED BY COLBY, WHO SIGNS AT HOME EARLY IN DAY

50 = Year Struggle Ends in Victory for Women

PROCLAMATION ENFRANCHISES WOMEN OF U. S.

NO CEREMONY IN FINAL ACTION

Secretary Felicitates Leaders; Hails New Era.

Bainbridge Colby, Secretary of State of the United States of America.

To all to whom these presents shall come, greeting:

Know ye, that the Congress of the United States at the first session, Sixty-sixth Congress, begun at Washington on the nineteenth day of May, in the year one thousand nine hundred and nineteen, passed a resolution as follows, to wit:

Joint resolution, proposing an amendment to the Constitution extending the right of suffrage to women

Ratification of th...

Alice Paul

"There will never be a new world order until women are a part of it."

Alice Paul knew how to put social issues in the public spotlight. Paul was a suffragist, a bold leader, and a fighter.

Paul once worked with Carrie Chapman Catt on their shared goal of equality for women. But Paul thought NAWSA needed more forceful tactics. She wanted to focus on getting President Woodrow Wilson on their side.

Paul's Battle

Even after the Nineteenth Amendment passed, Paul kept fighting for women's rights. The right to vote did not stop discrimination. In 1923, Paul wrote the first draft of the Equal Rights Amendment. She wrote it to ensure equal opportunities and rights for all. She spent the rest of her life pushing for it to be passed.

Parade of Support

Paul's picketing of the White House was not the first time she promoted women's rights in such a public way. March 3, 1913, was the day before Wilson was sworn in as president. Paul arranged a parade of more than 5,000 women to march from the U.S. Capitol to the White House. The publicity brought attention to the suffragist cause.

▲ Suffragists protest outside the White House in 1917.

Paul left NAWSA. Eventually, she founded the National Woman's Party and took the fight to the White House. Starting in 1917, Paul and her followers **picketed** the White House. They were the first people ever to do so. They were called "Silent Sentinels" because they stood outside and did not speak. Over one thousand people marched and waved banners. "Mr. President, How Long Must Women Wait For Liberty?" the banners asked.

When World War I began, the situation grew tense. The picketing was seen as unpatriotic. Paul was thrown in jail. But even in prison, Paul protested. She went on a hunger strike. Reporters soon heard of Paul's story. Her situation won public sympathy for the cause. Finally, in 1918, President Wilson announced his support for the suffrage movement.

Paul played a huge role in the fight for women's rights. It was a fight she continued to her final days.

The Change Makers

They were presidents and muckrakers, reformers and suffragists. All came from different walks of life. Everyone had their own dreams and ambitions. But they were all dedicated to the causes of the Progressive Era.

Lasting from 1890 to 1920, this era brought about a number of reforms. The government made a big shift toward working for its people. Labor laws were put in place. Food became more sanitary. Trusts were broken apart. Factories had to improve their working conditions. Women won the right to vote. The Fed started keeping the banks in check. Serious talks about civil rights began.

◄ Paul holds a flag with 36 stars—one for each state that ratified the Nineteenth Amendment.

A lot of progress was tucked into these 30 years. This progress was due to the hard work and dedication of the Progressive Era's leaders. Reading about them provides only a piece of the overall story. Their lives are powerful reminders of how people can shape their world—and the future.

▼ **Meatpacking workers march in a Labor Day parade.**

The Roaring Twenties

The 1920s were full of jazz and big social changes. For the first time in American history, there were more people living in cities than in the countryside. People were wealthier, women felt freer, and planes began to glide high in the sky. The Roaring Twenties, as the time came to be known, was an era that sizzled and soared.

Two More Amendments

Two more amendments were added to the Constitution during this time. Both came in 1913. The Sixteenth allowed a tax on people's incomes. The Seventeenth allowed voters to choose their own state senators. This helped weed out corruption from big business influences.

Track It!

The people in this book had some of the most powerful voices in the Progressive Era. Their accomplishments changed their country. Using the text, as well as independent research, create a Progressive Era time line. Track how all these different life stories intertwined over the years.

Make sure your time line does the following:

- ★ begins in 1890 and ends in 1920
- ★ includes major events of the suffragist movement, trust-busting, and other reform activities
- ★ mentions specific dates (day, month, year)

Have fun with your time line! Think of a unique and creative way to track the Progressive Era. You can present the time line as any of these options:

- ★ individual cards clipped on a laundry line
- ★ an interactive experience using a website
- ★ a series of photographs of major events
- ★ or something else entirely!

Glossary

amendment—a change or an addition made to the Constitution

complacent—satisfied with how things are and not wanting to change them

conglomerate—a large business made up of different kinds of companies

exploitation—the act of using someone unfairly for one's own advantage

exposés—news reports or broadcasts that reveal illegal or dishonest things to the public

idealist—a person who believes it is possible to live by high standards of behavior

injustice—unfair treatment of a person or group of people

innovation—the act or process of introducing new ideas, devices, or methods

mediated—worked with opposite sides to reach an agreement

monopolies—single companies or individuals who have complete control over entire supplies of goods or services

movements—series of organized actions in which large groups of people work together to achieve something

nonpartisan—not supporting any political party

picketed—held signs and marched outside a place to protest something

ratified—made official by signing or voting

reforms—changes made to something to improve it

regulations—rules or laws that say how something should be done

repealed—officially made no longer valid or the law

serial—a story that is released in parts and with a certain frequency

suffrage—the right to vote in elections

trusts—groups of companies that work together to try to control industries by getting rid of competition

unethical—morally bad

Index

Your Turn!

A great deal of change happened during the Progressive Era. These changes were big news and written about in newspapers. Learn more about one of the Progressive Era causes that are in this book. Then, find out about a major event that took place related to that cause, such as a strike, protest, or vote. Finally, write a newspaper article about the event. Give facts and quotations from important people. Remember, newspaper articles should be based in fact, not opinion or bias. Include a primary source image to support your article.